I0407644

THINKING LIKE AN

ENTREPRENEUR

Mastering The Entrepreneurial Mindset

For Success and Innovation

Daryl Cass

TABLE OF CONTENTS

INTRODUCTION

In an ever-evolving world brimming with boundless opportunities, the entrepreneurial spirit stands tall as the driving force behind innovation, growth, and transformation. Entrepreneurs possess a unique mindset, an insatiable hunger for success, and an unwavering belief in their abilities to reshape the world around them. But what sets these visionaries apart? What enables them to navigate the tumultuous seas of uncertainty and emerge victorious?

Welcome to "Thinking Like an Entrepreneur,"an immersive journey that transcends the boundaries of traditional business literature. This book is an exploration of the profound mindset, strategies, and principles that empower entrepreneurs to turn mere ideas into thriving ventures. Whether you're a budding entrepreneur, a seasoned business professional, or an individual seeking to enhance your problem-solving abilities and unlock untapped potential, this book serves as your trusted guide.

Chapter by chapter, we will dive deep into the psyche of successful entrepreneurs, dissecting their thought processes, and unveiling the secret ingredients that fuel their relentless pursuit of greatness. Drawing upon real-life experiences, time-tested strategies, and cutting-edge research, this book equips you with the tools you need to embrace the entrepreneurial mindset and apply it to your own life, regardless of your chosen path.

In these pages, you'll uncover how to identify opportunities where others see obstacles, cultivate resilience in the face of adversity, and craft innovative solutions to society's most pressing challenges. You'll learn to harness the power of strategic thinking, turning ambiguity into clarity, and transforming risks into calculated leaps of faith.

We will explore the critical skills that entrepreneurs embody, such as effective decision-making, agile problem-solving, and adaptability in the face of ever-changing market dynamics. Together, we will unravel the mysteries behind nurturing an entrepreneurial spirit, fostering creativity, and building robust networks that fuel collaborative innovation.

But this book is more than a mere compilation of theories and concepts. It's an interactive companion, offering practical exercises, thought-provoking reflections, and actionable steps that encourage you to apply the principles directly to your own life and work. Each chapter will challenge your preconceptions, provoke introspection, and inspire you to push beyond your limits.

So, whether you're an aspiring entrepreneur on the cusp of launching your venture or an individual eager to embrace an entrepreneurial mindset in your personal and professional life, "Thinking Like an Entrepreneur"will be your steadfast companion on this transformative journey. Together, we will unlock the secrets to mastering strategic thinking, seizing opportunities, and carving your own path towards success in an ever-changing world.

Now, fasten your seatbelt, open your mind to the possibilities that lie ahead, and get ready to unleash your inner entrepreneur like never before. The adventure begins now.

CHAPTER 1

UNDERSTANDING THE
ENTREPRENEURIAL MINDSET

The Entrepreneurial mentality is a surprising condition of reasoning that separates effective business visionaries from the group. It incorporates a one of a kind mix of qualities, perspectives, and abilities that engage people to recognize open doors, proceed with reasonable plans of action, and change thoughts into effective endeavors. In this extensive investigation, we will dig profound into the complexities of the pioneering attitude, unwinding its center components and revealing insight into how it shapes the activities and results of the people who embrace it.

Visionary Reasoning:

At the core of the innovative outlook lies visionary reasoning. Business people have the capacity to see past the present, imagining a future that is not the same as the norm. They distinguish holes on the lookout, expect to arise drifts, and conceptualize creative answers to address neglected issues. This forward-looking point of view drives their energy and fills their determined quest for their objectives.

Embracing Hazard and Vulnerability:

Business visionaries are OK with vulnerability and embrace risk as a fundamental piece of the excursion. They comprehend that wandering into unfamiliar domains conveys intrinsic dangers, however they view these dangers as any open doors for development and learning. As opposed to being incapacitated by dread, they compute gambles, settle on informed choices, and view disappointments as venturing stones toward possible achievement.

Flexibility and Tirelessness:

Flexibility is a foundation of the pioneering mentality. Business people face various snags, misfortunes, and disappointments on their excursion. Notwithstanding, they have the capacity to quickly return from misfortune, gain from their mix-ups, and persist in spite of difficulties. Their faithful assurance and steadiness empower them to remain fixed on their objectives, continually adjusting and repeating until they accomplish their ideal results.

Imaginative Critical thinking:

Business visionaries are regular issue solvers. They have an imaginative and creative mentality that permits them to move toward difficulties from exceptional points. They question suspicions, rock the boat, and search out offbeat arrangements. By considering some fresh possibilities and embracing a development mentality, business visionaries disturb enterprises, present earth shattering items and administrations, and make new market spaces.

Energy and Reason:

Energy and objects are the main impetus behind the enterprising attitude. Business people are profoundly enthusiastic about their thoughts, items, or causes. They are filled by a deep yearning to have a significant effect and leave an enduring inheritance. This energy drives them through the high points and low points of the enterprising excursion, filling in as a consistent wellspring of inspiration and motivation.

Persistent Learning and Versatility:

Business visionaries perceive that learning is a long lasting interaction. They have an unquenchable hunger for information and are ceaselessly looking for chances to grow their ranges of abilities and expand their points of view. They are versatile and spry, promptly embracing change and utilizing new advancements and patterns for their potential benefit. By remaining on the ball, business people stay significant and receptive to advancing business sector elements.

Proactive and Activity Situated:

Business visionaries are not happy with basically ideating; they are headed to make a move. They have a predisposition for activity, utilizing their enterprising mentality to transform thoughts into the real world. Instead of hanging tight for the ideal second or every one of the responses, they proceed with carefully thought out plans of action and get things going. Business visionaries comprehend that headway is made through activity, and they won't hesitate to focus in and take care of business.

Viable Correspondence and Initiative:

Fruitful business visionaries have solid correspondence and authority abilities. They can express their vision, move others, and fabricate high-performing groups. They grasp the significance of joint effort, appointment, and engaging others to accomplish shared objectives. By developing viable relational abilities, business people make a culture of advancement, sustain connections, and draw in assets to help their endeavors.

Constancy Despite Disappointment:

Disappointment is an unavoidable piece of the innovative excursion. Nonetheless, business visionaries view disappointment as a potential chance to learn, develop, and turn. They have a development mentality that permits them to extricate significant examples from misfortunes and use them to fuel future achievement. As opposed to surrendering, they continue, adjust, and emphasize until they track down the correct way ahead.

Systems administration and Building Connections:

Business people perceive the force of organizations and connections. They effectively search out coaches, consultants, and similar people who can give direction, backing, and admittance to assets. By building solid connections, business people tap into an abundance of information, open doors, and coordinate efforts that speed up their development and increment their odds of coming out on top.

An enterprising mentality is a strong power that drives development, development, and positive change. Understanding the complexities of this mentality is fundamental for anybody trying to leave on a pioneering venture or develop an innovative soul. By embracing visionary reasoning, embracing risk, cultivating strength, and improving their critical thinking abilities, people can open their maximum capacity and have a significant effect in their chosen fields. The innovative mentality isn't restricted to business people alone; an outlook can be embraced by any individual who tries to imagine something truly mind-blowing, make a move, and make a superior future.

CHAPTER 2

IDENTIFYING OPPORTUNITIES

At the center of the pioneering venture
lies the specialty of distinguishing
potential open doors in the midst of an
ocean of conceivable outcomes. Business
visionaries have a special capacity to see
what others ignore, reveal stowed away
potential, and exploit arising patterns.
They have a sharp feeling of perception,
an inquisitive brain, and an unflinching
conviction that each issue holds the seed
of chance. In this part, we will investigate
the complexities of recognizing valuable

open doors, analyzing the mentality, systems, and techniques that engage business people to jump all over the opportunity and make extraordinary endeavors.

Embracing an Oddity Driven Mentality:

Effective business visionaries have a voracious interest, continually trying to figure out their general surroundings. They clarify pressing issues, challenge suspicions, and effectively draw in with their current circumstance. By keeping an open and responsive mentality, business visionaries reveal stowed associations, spot arising patterns, and distinguish holes in the market that others disregard. They view each experience as an expected wellspring of motivation and endeavor to stay at the front of information in their field.

Dissecting Business Sector Patterns and Purchaser Needs:

Business people have a profound comprehension of market elements and purchaser needs. They direct careful statistical surveying, dissect drifts, and distinguish holes in the current contributions. By concentrating on customer conduct, inclinations, and trouble spots, business visionaries can recognize neglected needs and plan creative arrangements. They submerge themselves in the objective market, gain experiences into client wants, and design their items or administrations to address explicit trouble spots successfully.

Utilizing Innovation and Interruption:

Innovative progressions and problematic powers make prolific ground for pioneering open doors. Business people stay receptive to arising advancements, like man-made brainpower, blockchain, or the Web of Things. They perceive the possible effect of these innovations on different ventures and imagine how they can use them to make new items, administrations, or plans of action. By embracing disturbance, business people position themselves at the bleeding edge of progress and saddle the force of mechanical headways to drive development.

Tackling Issues and Tending to Problem Areas:

Business visionaries are normal issue solvers. They recognize difficulties and trouble spots looked by people, organizations, or society all in all. By sympathizing with the battles of others, business visionaries track down potential chances to give arrangements that mitigate these problem areas. They listen mindfully, notice, and participate in discussions to acquire bits of knowledge into the issues individuals face. By offering successful and special arrangements, business visionaries cut out their specialty and make an incentive for their clients.

Systems Administration and Building Connections:

Open doors frequently arise through associations and connections. Business visionaries effectively develop networks, construct associations with vital participants in their industry, and search out tutors and counsels who can give direction and backing. By partaking in industry occasions, joining proficient networks, and utilizing the influence of informal organizations, business people get close enough to an abundance of data, assets, and joint effort open doors. These connections frequently lead to fortunate experiences and important associations that open ways to new open doors.

Embracing a Worldwide Viewpoint:

Business visionaries think past nearby limits and embrace a worldwide point of view. They perceive that open doors can emerge from worldwide patterns, developing business sectors, or multifaceted coordinated efforts. By keeping a finger on the beat of worldwide turns of events, business visionaries recognize undiscovered business sectors, influence social variety, and benefit from worldwide changes in buyer conduct. They comprehend the force of globalization and position themselves to jump all over chances on a worldwide scale.

Continually Developing and Emphasizing:

Business people comprehend that recognizing valuable open doors is a continuous interaction. They are focused on ceaseless advancement and cycle. They continually check the climate, screen market drifts, and adjust to changing client needs. By encouraging a culture of trial and error and embracing a development outlook, business visionaries stay on the ball and guarantee that their items, administrations, or plans of action stay pertinent in a quickly developing scene.

Embracing Disappointment as An Open Door:

Business people perceive that disappointment is an unavoidable piece of the pioneering venture. They view disappointment as a significant learning opportunity as opposed to a detour. Every misfortune gives bits of knowledge and illustrations that shape how they might interpret the market and guide them toward future open doors. Business people embrace disappointment, gain from it, and turn while essential, guaranteeing that misfortunes become venturing stones on their way to progress.

Natural and Social Awareness:

The present business visionaries are progressively determined by a feeling of ecological and social obligation. They recognize chances to resolve squeezing cultural issues, like maintainability, correspondence, or admittance to training and medical care. By adjusting their dares to a bigger reason, business visionaries make organizations that produce benefits as well as have a constructive outcome on the world. They perceive that open doors lie in monetary profits as well as in making a superior future for people and networks.

Recognizing open doors is an expertise sharpened by business visionaries through a blend of mentality, market examination, development, and versatility. By embracing interest, remaining sensitive to showcase patterns, utilizing innovation, and taking care of issues, business people uncover pathways to progress. They assemble networks, think all around the world, embrace disappointment, and remain earth and socially cognizant. Distinguishing open doors is a continuous cycle, and business visionaries persistently develop their viewpoints and techniques to explore an always evolving scene. With a sharp eye, a receptive outlook, and a steady drive to make esteem, business visionaries quickly jump all over the opportunity and change potential open doors into flourishing endeavors that shape their general surroundings.

CHAPTER 3

EMBRACING RISKS AND FAILURES

Hazard and disappointment are two indistinguishable buddies on the enterprising excursion. While many might see them as impediments, effective business visionaries view them as impetus for development and learning. Business visionaries have a novel mentality that empowers them to embrace gambles, explore vulnerability, and change disappointments into significant venturing stones towards progress. In this section, we will investigate the significant connection between business, risk-taking, and disappointment, revealing the procedures and viewpoints that engage business people to flourish despite difficulty.

Reasonable Courses of Action Taking:

Business visionaries comprehend that hazard is an innate piece of any pioneering try. Be that as it may, they are not wild speculators; all things considered, they participate in reasonable courses of action taking. They evaluate likely dangers, lead intensive statistical surveying, and go with informed choices in light of accessible data. Business people influence their insight, experience, and instinct to think about the possible prizes in contrast to the related dangers. By proceeding with carefully weighed out courses of action, business visionaries position themselves for critical increases while limiting likely misfortunes.

Embracing Vulnerability:

Vulnerability is the jungle gym of business visionaries. Rather than being deadened by the obscure, they embrace it as a chance for development. Business visionaries comprehend that vulnerability frequently goes with advancement and disturbance. They flourish in conditions where others waver, perceiving that the best leap forwards happen while venturing beyond safe places. By embracing vulnerability, business visionaries encourage imagination, flexibility, and an outlook that invites change.

Gaining from Disappointment:

Disappointment isn't an end for business visionaries; it is an important instructor. Business visionaries view disappointment as a fundamental piece of the growing experience. They perceive that mishaps give important bits of knowledge, offering illustrations that shape their future choices and methodologies. Rather than harping on disappointments, business people investigate their slips up, distinguish regions for development, and apply newly discovered information to their next adventures. By reexamining disappointment as learning an open door, business visionaries construct flexibility, adjust their methodologies, and increment their possibilities of future achievement.

Fostering a Development Outlook:

Business visionaries have a development mentality, which is established in the conviction that capacities can be created through commitment and difficult work. They view moves and disappointments as open doors to learn, develop, and advance. Rather than surrendering to self-question, business visionaries keep an uplifting perspective and spotlight on consistent improvement. They comprehend that difficulties are brief and that steadiness is fundamental notwithstanding affliction. By embracing a development outlook, business visionaries foster the versatility and persistence expected to defeat deterrents and accomplish their objectives.

Cycle and Flexibility:

Business visionaries are not limited by inflexible plans or fixed procedures. They comprehend that the enterprising excursion is a dynamic and developing interaction. Business visionaries embrace adaptability, permitting them to adjust to changing economic situations, client inclinations, and arising patterns. They emphasize their items, administrations, and plans of action in view of criticism and market reaction. By embracing flexibility, business people stay responsive, agile, and equipped for taking advantage of new chances as they emerge.

Risk Relief Methodologies:

Business people are not risk-opposed; they are risk chiefs. They utilize different systems to alleviate possible dangers and safeguard their endeavors. Business visionaries take part in situation arranging, directing exhaustive gamble appraisals and creating alternate courses of action. They broaden their income streams, lay areas of strength for out, and assemble vigorous organizations that offer help and assets in the midst of vulnerability. By executing risk the board procedures, business visionaries limit expected harm and increment their capacity to recuperate from mishaps.

Embracing the Feeling of Dread Toward Lament:

Business visionaries frequently experience the apprehension about lament, which inspires them to face challenges and seek after their enterprising dreams. They perceive that the lament of not attempting offsets the feeling of dread toward disappointment. Business people figure out that leaving nothing to chance and adhering to the state of affairs can prompt a long period of unfulfilled potential. By embracing the apprehension about lament, business visionaries track down the mental fortitude to step outside their usual ranges of familiarity and seek after amazing open doors that can prompt remarkable accomplishments.

Emotionally Supportive Networks and Guides:

Business visionaries perceive the significance of a solid emotionally supportive network and look for direction from guides and consultants. They encircle themselves with similar people who share their energy and drive. Coaches give significant bits of knowledge, share encounters, and proposition direction through the highs and lows of the pioneering venture. By resting on emotionally supportive networks and guides, business people gain the certainty and consolation expected to embrace gambles and explore the difficulties of business ventures.

Observing Little Wins:

Business visionaries celebrate little wins en route, perceiving that achievement isn't exclusively characterized by accomplishing a definitive objective. They recognize and value progress, regardless of how steady. By celebrating little wins, business people stay roused, keep up with force, and develop a positive mentality. This energy gives the versatility expected to continue on through disappointments and mishaps, at last prompting long haul achievement.

Embracing dangers and disappointment is a central part of reasoning like a business visionary. Business visionaries comprehend that risk-taking is a fundamental element for development and advancement. By embracing vulnerability, gaining from disappointment, and taking on a development mentality, business people change mishaps into venturing stones toward progress. They foster methodologies to moderate dangers, look for direction from coaches, and fabricate an emotionally supportive network that urges them to endure regardless of difficulties. With each determined gamble taken, and with every disappointment experienced, business visionaries become stronger, versatile, and better prepared to immediately jump all over the chances that lie ahead.

CHAPTER 4

DEVELOPING AN EFFECTIVE
BUSINESS STRATEGY

Thinking like a business person goes past ideation and hazard taking; it requires the capacity to create and execute successful business techniques. Business people have an exceptional insight for adjusting their vision, objectives, and assets to make a guide that prompts achievement. In this part, we will investigate the workmanship and study of creating viable business methodologies, looking at the key components, systems, and approaches that engage business visionaries to explore the intricacies of the business scene and accomplish their goals.

Characterizing Vision and Mission:

Successful business systems start with an unmistakable vision and mission. Business people articulate their drawn out yearnings and characterize the reason that drives their endeavors. They lay out a convincing vision that motivates partners and makes an internal compass. The statement of purpose embodies the fundamental beliefs, objectives, and techniques that guide the association's exercises. By characterizing areas of strength for a mission, business visionaries establish the groundwork for creating techniques that line up with their general reason.

Directing Complete Marke Examination:

Effective business visionaries figure out the significance of careful market examination. They survey the cutthroat scene, recognize market drifts, and assess client requirements and inclinations. By leading statistical surveying, business people gain bits of knowledge into buyer conduct, market elements, and arising potential open doors. This information fills in as a reason for figuring out procedures that influence market experiences and make an upper hand.

Laying out Savvy Objectives:

Successful business methodologies are based upon explicit, quantifiable, reachable, applicable, and time-bound (Shrewd) objectives. Business people separate their vision into significant goals that are sensible and lined up with their assets. Shrewd objectives give a reasonable concentration, empower following advancement, and encourage responsibility. By putting forth obvious objectives, business visionaries guarantee that their procedures are deliberate and quantifiable, prompting unmistakable results.

Distinguishing Objective Market and Client Fragments:

Business people perceive the significance of characterizing their objective market and recognizing explicit client fragments. They comprehend that a one-size-fits-all approach is seldom powerful. All things considered, business visionaries lead market division, recognizing unmistakable gatherings of clients with interesting necessities, inclinations, and ways of behaving. By understanding their objective market and client fragments, business visionaries tailor their systems to address the particular requests of each gathering really.

Separation and Incentive:

Fruitful business visionaries foster a convincing incentive that separates their contributions from rivals. They distinguish their interesting selling focuses and convey the worth they give to clients. By zeroing in on separation, business visionaries make an upper hand that draws in clients and fabricates brand steadfastness. The offer turns into a core value in planning techniques that feature the particular advantages their items or administrations offer.

Creating a Versatile Plan of Action:

Business people comprehend the significance of planning a versatile plan of action. They survey the practicality of their thoughts and assess their capacity to create reasonable income and development. By fostering a versatile plan of action, business people formulate procedures that permit them to grow and adjust to changing economic situations. They distinguish income streams, cost designs, and key associations that help long haul productivity and adaptability.

Evaluating and Overseeing Dangers:

Business visionaries adopt a proactive strategy to gamble with evaluation and the executives. They distinguish possible dangers and foster procedures to moderate or limit them. Business visionaries lead exhaustive gamble investigation, taking into account interior and outside factors that might influence their endeavors. They make emergency courses of action, expand their assets, and influence their organization to address expected difficulties. By actually overseeing gambles, business visionaries increment their odds of coming out on top and guarantee the supportability of their endeavors.

Forming Advertising and Deals Methodologies:

Business people perceive that viable promoting and deals techniques are pivotal for business development. They foster thorough advertising plans that focus on their distinguished client sections. They influence different channels, like advanced promoting, virtual entertainment, or customary publicizing, to successfully contact their crowd. Business visionaries likewise plan deals procedures that line up with their objective market and incentive, guaranteeing that their contributions reverberate with clients and drive income development.

Constructing High-Performing Groups:

Business people comprehend that a solid group is instrumental in executing business techniques successfully. They center around recruiting skilled people who line up with their vision and mission. Business visionaries cultivate a culture of joint effort, persistent learning, and development inside their associations. They engage their groups, give clear heading, and establish a climate that supports imagination and development. By building high-performing groups, business visionaries improve their capacity to execute systems and accomplish their objectives.

Constant Assessment and Transformation:

Business people perceive that techniques should be persistently assessed and adjusted to stay significant and compelling. They lay out key execution pointers (KPIs) to gauge progress and achievement. Business people examine information, assemble criticism, and look for bits of knowledge to evaluate the effect of their techniques. They stay coordinated, making important changes and turns in light of economic situations and developing client needs. By embracing a persistent assessment and variation outlook, business visionaries guarantee their procedures stay dynamic and lined up with their objectives.

Creating compelling business procedures is a fundamental part of reasoning like a business person. Business people join vision, market examination, objective setting, and separation to create procedures that lead to progress. By distinguishing objective business sectors, making a convincing incentive, and planning versatile plans of action, business visionaries position themselves for development and productivity. They evaluate and oversee chances, figure out advertising and deals procedures, and assemble high-performing groups to actually execute their arrangements. Through ceaseless assessment and transformation, business visionaries stay receptive to advertise elements, guaranteeing their systems stay powerful and lined up with their drawn out goals. By excelling at creating viable business procedures, business people lay the preparation for building effective endeavors and having an enduring effect in their picked ventures.

CHAPTER 5

BUILDING A STRONG NETWORK
AND COLLABORATION

Thinking like a business person goes past individual splendor; it envelops the capacity to fabricate areas of strength for an and cultivate cooperative connections. Effective business people comprehend the force of associations and the worth of coordinated effort in exploring the intricacies of the business scene. In this section, we will investigate the significance of building areas of strength for an and developing cooperative organizations, uncovering the methodologies, advantages, and approaches that engage business visionaries to flourish in an interconnected world.

The Benefit of Systems Administration:

Organizing is a foundation of enterprising achievement. Business people comprehend that building major areas of strength gives admittance to assets, mastery, and potential open doors. They effectively search out systems administration occasions, industry meetings, and networks where they can associate with similar people. By extending their organization, business visionaries tap into an abundance of information, backing, and potential coordinated efforts that fuel their development and entryways to new pursuits.

Making Significant Connections:

Business people center around making significant connections as opposed to simple shallow associations. They approach organizing with credibility and a veritable interest in others. Business people effectively tune in, participate in discussions, and look to figure out the necessities and yearnings of their organization. By building trust and sustaining connections, business visionaries lay out an establishment for joint effort and backing that reaches out past simple expert corporations.

Utilizing Online Entertainment and Computerized Stages:

In the present advanced age, business visionaries influence web-based entertainment and computerized stages to grow their organization and enhance their span. They use stages like LinkedIn, Twitter, and industry-explicit gatherings to associate with experts, share experiences, and take part in discussions. By utilizing computerized stages, business people rise above topographical limits and associate with people from different foundations and skill, growing their organization universally.

Participating in Local Area Association:

Business people effectively take part in local area association, perceiving that it cultivates significant associations and improves their standing. They partake in industry affiliations, volunteer for local area drives, and backing causes lined up with their qualities. By taking part in local area contribution, business people construct a positive brand picture, lay out believability, and set out open doors for joint effort and backing inside their local area.

Looking for Tutors and Guides:

Fruitful business visionaries look for direction from guides and counsels who give significant experiences and backing. They recognize people who have made progress in their field or have particular information pertinent to their industry. Business visionaries take part in mentorship programs, look for casual mentorship connections, or join pioneering networks that work with mentorship associations. By gaining from experienced tutors, business people get close enough to insight, keep away from normal entanglements, and speed up their development.

Shaping Vital Organizations:

Business visionaries comprehend the force of vital organizations in extending their range and getting to new open doors. They look for joint efforts with corresponding organizations or people who share comparable qualities and objectives. Business people search for collaborations and chances to consolidate assets, mastery, and organizations to make shared benefits. By shaping vital associations, business people influence aggregate qualities, increment their market reach, and tackle difficulties that would be hard to independently survive.

Encouraging a Cooperative Culture:

Business people develop a cooperative culture inside their associations and organizations. They cultivate a climate where thoughts are shared, input is invited, and coordinated effort is empowered. Business visionaries perceive that assorted points of view and interdisciplinary joint efforts can prompt inventive arrangements and new open doors. By cultivating a cooperative culture, business people saddle the aggregate insight of their organization and make a biological system of help and development.

Co-making with Clients and Partners:

Business people effectively include clients and partners in the co-creation process. They look for criticism, pay attention to client experiences, and draw in them in items or administration advancement. Business visionaries view clients as accomplices and partners, esteeming their commitments and including them in direction. By co-making with clients and partners, business visionaries guarantee that their contributions line up with market needs, improve consumer loyalty, and drive development.

Building a Strong Biological System:

Business people perceive the force of a strong biological system that supports cooperation and development. They effectively add to the innovative local area by sharing information, offering help, and offering mentorship hoping for business visionaries. Business people take part in startup hatcheries, cooperating spaces, and industry-explicit organizations, establishing a climate where thoughts are traded, joint efforts are shaped, and aggregate achievement is praised.

Embracing Variety and Consideration:

Business people comprehend that variety and incorporation cultivate development and imagination. They effectively look for assorted points of view and embrace people from various foundations, societies, and encounters. Business visionaries perceive that different groups and organizations bring new bits of knowledge, challenge presumptions, and cultivate inventiveness. By embracing variety and incorporation, business visionaries make a rich embroidery of thoughts and coordinated efforts that drive enterprising achievement.

Building serious areas of strength for an and encouraging cooperation is indispensable to thinking like a business visionary. By effectively captivating in systems administration, making significant connections, and utilizing computerized stages, business visionaries extend their venture and tap into an abundance of assets and open doors. They look for direction from tutors, structure key associations, and co-make with clients and partners to drive advancement and development. By encouraging a cooperative culture, embracing variety, and effectively adding to the enterprising biological system, business visionaries fabricate an encouraging group of people that energizes their prosperity. Through the force of associations and joint effort, business visionaries enhance their effect, quickly jump all over new chances, and make an enduring heritage in their chosen fields.

CHAPTER 6

TAKING ACTIONS AND EXECUTING IDEAS

Thinking like a business visionary isn't restricted to ideation and vital preparation; it requires the capacity to make an unequivocal move and execute thoughts really. Effective business people comprehend that making a move is fundamental for transforming their vision into an unmistakable reality. In this section, we will investigate the significance of making a move and executing thoughts, looking at the outlook, systems, and practices that engage business visionaries to beat hindrances, explore difficulties, and change their pioneering dreams into fruitful endeavors.

Embracing an Inclination for Activity:

Business people have an inclination for activity; they are not satisfied with basically thinking and arranging. They comprehend that advancement and achievement are the aftereffects of making a conscious and reliable move. Business people defeat the feeling of dread toward disappointment and embrace the vulnerability that goes with the innovative excursion. By effectively chasing after their objectives, business visionaries make energy, jump all over chances, and gain unmistakable headway towards their ideal results.

Separating Objectives into Noteworthy Stages:

Fruitful business visionaries separate their objectives into significant stages. They make a guide that frames the essential activities to move from ideation to execution. By separating complex targets into more modest, reasonable assignments, business people try not to feel overpowered and increment their concentration and efficiency. This approach permits business visionaries to gain ground steadily, guaranteeing they remain focused towards their bigger objectives.

Building a Culture of Execution:

Business people encourage a culture of execution inside their associations and groups. They establish a climate where activity is esteemed, and thoughts are rejuvenated. Business visionaries urge their colleagues to take possession, decide, and execute their thoughts with independence. By cultivating a culture of execution, business people guarantee that thoughts are not left lethargic yet changed into substantial outcomes that move the association forward.

Embracing Emphasis and Variation:

Business people comprehend that execution is an iterative interaction. They perceive the need to adjust and turn in view of market criticism, client experiences, and evolving conditions. Business visionaries are able to gain from mix-ups and embrace a ceaseless improvement mentality. By repeating and adjusting their thoughts, business people refine their procedures, items, or administrations to more readily address the issues of their interest group and augment their odds of coming out on top.

Conquering Investigation Loss of Motion:

Business visionaries try not to fall into the snare of investigation loss of motion, where extreme preparation and overthinking obstruct progress. They figure out that making a move, even with defective data, can prompt important experiences and open doors for course revision. Business people pursue choices in light of the most ideal that anyone could hope to find data, confiding in their instinct and experience. They embrace an outlook of learning through doing and view botches as important illustrations that add to their development and achievement.

Utilizing a Predisposition for Trial and Error:

Business people approach execution with a mentality of trial and error. They view each activity as a chance to test presumptions, accumulate information, and gain from the results. Business people take on an outlook of embracing disappointments as a piece of the trial and error process. By leading limited scope tests, business people approve their thoughts, recognize expected imperfections, and arrive at educated conclusions about the future bearing regarding their endeavors.

Creating Viable Using Time Effectively:

Business visionaries perceive the significance of compelling time usage in executing their thoughts. They focus on assignments, set cutoff times, and spotlight on exercises that affect their objectives. Business people delegate unimportant errands, influence innovation and devices to smooth out processes, and dispense with interruptions that block efficiency. By dealing with their time actually, business visionaries enhance their endeavors, guaranteeing that they gain ground towards their objectives reliably.

Embracing Joint Effort and Appointment:

Business visionaries grasp the force of coordinated effort and designation in executing thoughts. They encircle themselves with gifted people who can supplement their abilities and skills. Business people influence the qualities of their colleagues, allocate liabilities, and engage them to independently execute errands. By embracing cooperation and designation, business people influence the aggregate abilities of their group, empowering them to execute thoughts all the more proficiently and really.

Defeating Obstruction and Difficulties:

Business people perceive that executing thoughts isn't without its difficulties. They comprehend that mishaps and opposition are inescapable on the innovative excursion. Business visionaries embrace a critical thinking mentality, looking for clever fixes, and persisting even with difficulty. They are tough, versatile, and view difficulties as any open doors for development and learning. By conquering obstruction and difficulties, business people foster the determination and industriousness expected to carry their plans to completion.

Observing Achievements and Victories:

Business visionaries commend achievements and triumphs along the execution venture. They recognize and value progress, regardless of how little, and celebrate accomplishments with their colleagues. By commending achievements, business people encourage a feeling of achievement and inspiration inside their association. This encouraging feedback motivates progress with activity and builds up the conviction that execution is a fulfilling and satisfying cycle.

Making a move and executing thoughts is the sign of reasoning like a business visionary. Business people grasp the significance of embracing a predisposition for activity, separating objectives into noteworthy stages, and cultivating a culture of execution. They conquer examination loss of motion, embrace cycle and transformation, and influence trial and error to approve and refine their thoughts. Through viable use of time productively, cooperation, and assignment, business visionaries upgrade their endeavors and influence the aggregate qualities of their group. By defeating difficulties, commending achievements, and gaining from disappointments, business people change their dreams into unmistakable real factors. Through the force of execution, business people rejuvenate their thoughts, make an incentive for their clients, and have an enduring effect in their chosen ventures.

CHAPTER 7

FINANCIAL MANAGEMENT AND FUNDING

Thinking like a business visionary goes past ideation and execution; it envelops the capacity to oversee funds and secure subsidizing actually. Fruitful business visionaries comprehend the significance of monetary administration and the job it plays in the manageability and development of their endeavors. In this section, we will investigate the complexities of supporting administration and subsidizing, looking at the techniques, approaches, and assets that engage business people to explore the monetary scene and secure the fundamental money to fuel their pioneering desires.

Fostering a Monetary Arrangement:

Business visionaries start their supporting process by fostering an exhaustive monetary arrangement. They evaluate their subsidizing needs, conjecture incomes and costs, and lay out monetary objectives and achievements. By fostering a clear cut monetary arrangement, business people gain lucidity on their monetary prerequisites and set a guide for accomplishing their targets. This plan fills in as an establishment for drawing in financial backers, getting credits, and overseeing income successfully.

Bootstrapping and Self-Subsidizing:

Business people frequently start by bootstrapping and self-subsidizing their endeavors. They use individual reserve funds, charge cards, or advances to finance starting activities and item improvement. Bootstrapping permits business visionaries to keep up with command over their endeavors and exhibit their responsibility and confidence in their thoughts. It additionally fills in as confirmation of idea, making the endeavor more appealing to expected financial backers or loan specialists.

Looking for Outer Funding:

As adventures develop, business visionaries might have to look for outside funding to fuel extension, item improvement, or market section. They investigate different choices like funding, private supporters, crowdfunding, or business advances. Business visionaries research and assess the advantages and disadvantages of each subsidizing source, taking into account factors, for example, value weakening, reimbursement terms, and the arrangement of financial backer assumptions with their drawn out objectives.

Building Serious Areas of Strength for a Pitch:

Business people comprehend the significance of building areas of strength for a pitch that successfully conveys their incentive, market potential, and development procedure. They make a convincing story that reverberates with likely financial backers, featuring the uniqueness of their endeavor and its true capacity for monetary returns. Business people focus intensely on refining their pitch, setting up a compact and enticing show that catches the premium and certainty of financial backers.

Developing Associations with Financial Backers:

Effective business people perceive that raising support is definitely not a one-time occasion yet a continuous cycle. They proactively develop associations with expected financial backers, going to systems administration occasions, industry meetings, and pitch rivalries. Business people take part in follow-up gatherings, give standard updates, and look for criticism from financial backers. By sustaining connections, business people construct trust and lay out an organization of allies who can give important direction, presentations, and follow-on subsidizing.

Bootstrapping Procedures for Effectiveness:

In any event, while outside subsidizing is gotten, business people keep on embracing bootstrapping methodologies to enhance their monetary assets. They center around cost control, arrange good seller agreements, and execute lean functional practices. Business visionaries focus on income age and income of the executives, guaranteeing that their endeavors remain monetarily supportable. By taking on bootstrapping systems, business visionaries amplify their monetary productivity and decrease dependence on outside financing sources.

Monetary Determining and Chance Administration:

Business people perceive the significance of monetary anticipation and risk to the executives in their supporting process.

They foster monetary models and projections that record for various situations and possible dangers. Business visionaries recognize potential income holes, plan for possibilities, and carry out risk alleviation methodologies. By actually overseeing monetary dangers, business visionaries improve their capacity to subsidize, go with informed choices, and guarantee the drawn out monetary wellbeing of their endeavors.

Utilizing Government and Award Projects:

Business visionaries investigate government awards, endowments, and impetus programs that can give extra subsidizing support. They research accessible projects, qualification models, and application processes. Business visionaries tap into government assets, hatcheries, or gas pedals that offer monetary help, mentorship, and systems administration open doors. By utilizing government and award programs, business people expand their money sources and get sufficiently close to specific help administrations.

Building Monetary Aptitude:

Business people figure out the significance of building monetary aptitude or looking for proficient direction to deal with their funds really. They focus intensely on grasping fiscal summaries, key execution markers, and monetary proportions. Business people draw in with bookkeepers, monetary consultants, or tutors who can give direction on monetary preparation, charge improvement, and monetary revealing. By building monetary discernment, business visionaries pursue informed monetary choices, assess subsidizing open doors, and screen the monetary soundness of their endeavors.

Overseeing Financial backer Connections:

Whenever subsidizing is gotten, business visionaries center around overseeing financial backer connections really. They give normal updates on key achievements, monetary execution, and vital drives. Business people keep up with open lines of correspondence, address financial backer worries, and look for direction when required. By overseeing financial backer connections well, business people construct trust, access extra subsidizing rounds, and influence the skill and organizations of their financial backers.

Supporting administration and subsidizing are essential parts of reasoning like a business person. Effective business visionaries foster exhaustive monetary plans, bootstrap and look for outside funding in a calculated way, and construct solid financial backer pitches. They develop associations with financial backers, influence taxpayer supported initiatives, and take on bootstrapping systems for monetary productivity. Business visionaries focus on monetary gauging and risk the board, construct monetary skill, and oversee financial backer connections actually. Through compelling monetary administration and getting fitting financing, business visionaries guarantee the supportability and development of their endeavors, empowering them to transform their pioneering dreams into fruitful real factors.

CHAPTER 8

MARKETING AND BRANDING

Thinking like a business visionary envelops the capacity to market and fabricate areas of strength for a presence successfully. Fruitful business visionaries figure out the force of showcasing and marking in drawing in clients, separating their contributions, and laying out an upper hand. In this section, we will investigate the complexities of showcasing and marking, looking at the methodologies, standards, and practices that engage business people to make serious areas of strength for a presence, associate with their ideal interest group, and construct enduring brand dependability.

Figuring out the Significance of Marketing:

Business people perceive that promoting isn't just about selling items or administrations; it is tied in with making worth and building associations with clients. They comprehend the significance of promoting in arriving at their interest group, imparting their offer, and driving client commitment. By embracing showcasing as a basic piece of their innovative excursion, business people can successfully situate their contributions and gain an upper hand.

Directing Statistical Surveying:

Effective business visionaries direct intensive statistical surveying to grasp their main interest group, rivalry, and market elements. They dissect purchaser conduct, distinguish market patterns, and gain experiences into client requirements and inclinations. By directing statistical surveying, business people can tailor their showcasing procedures to really reach and resonate with their main interest group, guaranteeing their contributions line up with market requests.

Characterizing Serious Areas of Strength for a Suggestion:

Business people foster a convincing incentive that separates their contributions from rivals. They recognize the exceptional advantages their items or administrations give to clients and impart this offer successfully. By characterizing areas of strength for a recommendation, business visionaries catch the consideration of their main interest group, construct trust, and lay out an unmistakable situation on the lookout.

Building a Predictable Brand Character:

Business people comprehend the significance of building a predictable brand character that mirrors their qualities, character, and incentive. They make a brand personality that resounds with their ideal interest group and imparts their novel story. Business visionaries foster a brand technique that incorporates components like a logo, variety range, manner of speaking, and visual character. By building a predictable brand character, business visionaries make acknowledgment, fabricate trust, and lay out areas of strength for an association with their clients.

Creating a Coordinated Advertising Technique:

Business visionaries foster an incorporated advertising system that joins different channels and strategies to successfully arrive at their interest group. They influence a blend of on the web and disconnected promoting channels, for example, virtual entertainment, content showcasing, site improvement, email showcasing, advertising, and occasions. By making an incorporated showcasing procedure, business visionaries expand their compass, draw in with their crowd at various touchpoints, and make a durable brand insight.

Using Advanced Promoting:

Business people embrace the force of computerized showcasing to enhance their image presence and interface with their main interest group. They influence web-based entertainment stages, web crawler advertising, content showcasing, and force to be reckoned with associations to increment brand perceivability, drive site traffic, and produce leads. Business people screen advanced investigation, track key execution pointers, and streamline their computerized promoting endeavors to accomplish the most extreme effect.

Building Solid Client Connections:

Business people comprehend that building solid client connections is essential for long haul achievement. They focus on consumer loyalty, commitment, and maintenance. Business people execute client relationship the executives techniques, for example, customized correspondence, client input components, dedication programs, and extraordinary client assistance. By building solid client connections, business visionaries encourage brand dedication, create verbal references, and drive rehash business.

Utilizing Narrating:

Business people outfit the force of narrating to interface with their crowd on a profound level. They share their enterprising excursion, values, and the effect their items or administrations have on clients' lives. By utilizing narrating, business people make a credible and interesting brand story that reverberates with their main interest group, develops brand dedication, and separates their contributions from rivals.

Participating in Thought Authority:

Business visionaries position themselves as thought forerunners in their industry by sharing significant bits of knowledge and ability. They make content, for example, blog entries, articles, whitepapers, and recordings that offer some benefit to their interest group. Business people take part in industry occasions, talk at gatherings, and add to important distributions. By participating in thought administration, business visionaries assemble believability, extend their scope, and draw in clients who esteem their ability.

Observing and Estimating Showcasing Endeavors:

Business people figure out the significance of checking and estimating the viability of their showcasing endeavors. They track key execution pointers (KPIs, for example, site traffic, change rates, web-based entertainment commitment, and client procurement costs. Business visionaries examine information, accumulate criticism, and go with information driven choices to enhance their showcasing methodologies. By checking and estimating showcasing endeavors, business visionaries guarantee their assets are dispensed successfully, and their promoting exercises create a positive profit from speculation.

Promoting and marketing are essential parts of reasoning like a business visionary. Fruitful business visionaries comprehend the significance of advertising in arriving at their main interest group, conveying their offer, and driving client commitment. They fabricate a predictable brand personality, create an incorporated promoting system, and use computerized showcasing channels to expand their compass and effect. By building solid client connections, utilizing narrating, and taking part in thought authority, business people develop brand dependability and lay down a good foundation for themselves as confided in industry pioneers. Through checking and estimating promoting endeavors, business visionaries streamline their methodologies and guarantee a positive profit from speculation. By really showcasing and marking their contributions, business visionaries make areas of strength for a presence, draw in clients, and construct enduring brand reliability that drives their pioneering achievement.

CHAPTER 9

SCALING AND GROWTH

Thinking like a business visionary reaches out past sending off an endeavor; it includes the capacity to scale and accomplish reasonable development. Effective business people figure out the significance of scaling their activities, extending their span, and amplifying their effect. In this part, we will investigate the standards, procedures, and practices that engage business visionaries to imagine greater possibilities, jump all over development chances, and explore the intricacies of scaling their endeavors.

Embracing a Development Outlook:

Business people develop a development mentality that embraces open doors for extension and nonstop improvement. They are not happy with the state of affairs however continually look for ways of developing and scale their endeavors. Business visionaries view difficulties as venturing stones, adjust to changing business sector elements, and stay open to additional opportunities. By embracing a development outlook, business people make a rich ground for practical development and extension.

Defining a Reasonable Vision and Objectives:

Effective business people have a reasonable vision for scaling their endeavors. They articulate their drawn out objectives, characterize key execution pointers (KPIs), and create a guide to accomplish their goals. Business people impart their vision to their colleagues and partners, adjusting their endeavors towards a shared objective. By defining an unmistakable vision and objectives, business people make an establishment for vital direction and centered development.

Fortifying Functional Cycles:

Business people comprehend the significance of smoothing out and reinforcing functional cycles as they scale. They improve work processes, execute versatile frameworks, and robotize tedious assignments. Business people recruit and train capable people to deal with expanded responsibilities and guarantee smooth tasks. By reinforcing functional cycles, business visionaries increment effectiveness, diminish expenses, and lay the foundation for scaling their endeavors effectively.

Extending Business Sector Reach:

Business people look for chances to grow their market reach as they scale. They direct statistical surveying, distinguish new client fragments, and foster systems to target undiscovered business sectors. Business visionaries investigate geographic development, conveyance associations, or online stages to widen their client base. By extending market reach, business people open new learning experiences and expand income streams.

Putting Resources into Innovation:

Business people influence innovation to drive scaling and development. They put resources into adaptable programming, framework, and computerized apparatuses that empower productive activities and further developed client encounters. Business people bridle the force of information examination, computerization, and man-made brainpower to settle on informed choices and drive development. By putting resources into innovation, business visionaries gain an upper hand, upgrade versatility, and open new roads for development.

Building Key Associations:

Business people structure key organizations to speed up development and extend their capacities. They look for coordinated efforts with corresponding organizations, industry pioneers, or appropriation channels that can give admittance to new business sectors or assets. Business people lay out mutually advantageous organizations that influence aggregate qualities and make common worth. By building vital organizations, business people increment their market presence, tap into new client bases, and open development potential.

Developing Areas of Strength for a Culture:

Business people comprehend the significance of developing areas of strength for a culture that upholds development and draws in top ability. They encourage a culture of development, cooperation, and advancing inside their associations. Business people impart their qualities, support representative strengthening, and perceive and compensate for accomplishments. By developing areas of strength for a culture, business visionaries fabricate a roused labor force, encourage inventiveness, and drive supportable development.

Overseeing Monetary Assets:

Business people successfully deal with their monetary assets as they scale. They foster monetary models, break down income, and plan for the financing expected to help development drives. Business visionaries look for outer subsidizing, arrange ideal terms, and carry out monetary controls to guarantee monetary supportability. By overseeing monetary assets decisively, business visionaries fuel development, limit chances, and exploit open doors for extension.

Nonstop Learning and Variation:

Business visionaries embrace a culture of persistent learning and variation as they scale. They keep up to date with industry patterns, client inclinations, and arising advancements. Business visionaries investigate information, accumulate client input, and pursue information driven choices to refine their procedures. By embracing persistent learning and variation, business people stay dexterous, receptive to advertise changes, and fit for supporting long haul development.

Building a Versatile Initiative Group:

Business people perceive the significance of building a versatile initiative group that can drive development. They enlist skilled people, delegate liabilities, and engage their colleagues to take responsibility for regions. Business visionaries center around initiative, turn of events, mentorship, and ability maintenance techniques to sustain a high-performing group. By building a versatile initiative group, business people make an establishment for supported development, proficient direction, and successful execution.

Scaling and development are basic parts of reasoning like a business visionary.

Effective business visionaries embrace a development mentality, put forth clear dreams and objectives, and fortify functional cycles. They grow their market reach, put resources into innovation, and assemble vital associations. Business people develop serious areas of strength for a culture, successfully oversee monetary assets, and cultivate a culture of nonstop learning and variation. By building a versatile initiative group, business visionaries engage their associations to support development and expand their effect. Through essential reasoning, development, and the capacity to jump all over development chances, business people open their endeavors' actual potential and make an enduring imprint in the enterprising scene.

CHAPTER 10

CONTINUOUS LEARNING AND ADAPTATION

Thinking like a business visionary is an excursion of steady development and advancement. Effective business people comprehend the significance of consistent learning and variation notwithstanding a quickly changing business scene. In this section, we will investigate the standards, techniques, and practices that engage business people to embrace an outlook of ceaseless learning, adjust to showcase moves, and stay spray in their quest for progress.

Embracing a Development Mentality:

Business visionaries develop a development outlook that embraces constant learning and self-improvement. They view difficulties as any open doors for development and learning. Business visionaries search out new information, gain new abilities, and stay open to input and helpful analysis. By embracing a development mentality, business people encourage a feeling of interest, strength, and an eagerness to improve persistently.

Focusing on Long Lasting Learning:

Fruitful business visionaries focus on long lasting advancement as a center part of their enterprising excursion. They comprehend that information and abilities are not static however require progressing improvement. Business people participate in ceaseless schooling, go to courses, studios, and gatherings. They read books, pay attention to webcasts, and partake in web-based courses to remain informed and grow their skill. By focusing on long lasting learning, business visionaries stay on top of things and adjust to arising patterns and innovations.

Looking for Different Viewpoints:

Business visionaries perceive the benefit of looking for different points of view and encounters. They effectively search out various perspectives, participate in conversations, and encircle themselves with people from assorted foundations. Business visionaries comprehend that assorted viewpoints invigorate innovativeness, challenge suspicions, and cultivate advancement. By looking for assorted points of view, business visionaries expand their perspectives, gain new bits of knowledge, and upgrade their critical thinking capacities.

Adjusting to Market Movements:

Business people comprehend that market shifts are unavoidable. They stay careful and versatile to changing business sector elements, client needs, and arising innovations. Business people screen industry patterns, break down information, and accumulate client criticism to distinguish arising amazing open doors and expected dangers. By adjusting to advertise shifts, business visionaries position themselves to use recent fads and remain in front of the opposition.

Embracing Disappointment as a Learning, A valuable open door:

Business people embrace disappointment as a significant learning opportunity instead of a mishap. They view disappointments as venturing stones to progress and concentrate important examples from their encounters. Business visionaries dissect their disappointments, recognize regions for development, and change their systems as needs be. By embracing disappointment, business visionaries foster versatility, gain from their errors, and refine their methodologies.

Testing and Repeating:

Business visionaries figure out the significance of trial and error and cycle in their enterprising excursion. They won't hesitate to test novel thoughts, items, or systems. Business people take on an iterative methodology, looking for input from clients and partners to refine and work on their contributions. By testing and repeating, business visionaries reveal experiences, approve suppositions, and upgrade the worth they give to their ideal interest group.

Building an Organization of Coaches and Guides:

Fruitful business visionaries encircle themselves with coaches and counsels who can give direction and backing. They look for coaches who have applicable aptitude and can offer significant bits of knowledge. Business visionaries participate in mentorship programs, join pioneering organizations, and look for casual mentorship connections. By building an organization of tutors and counsels, business visionaries get close enough to shrewdness, experience, and points of view that speed up their learning and development.

Ceaseless Improvement of Cycles and Frameworks:

Business visionaries comprehend that consistent improvement is urgent for long haul achievement. They assess their cycles, frameworks, and tasks consistently to recognize failures and bottlenecks. Business visionaries influence innovation, robotization, and criticism systems to smooth out work processes and improve efficiency. By persistently further developing cycles and frameworks, business visionaries make a culture of productivity, viability, and development inside their associations.

Embracing New Innovations:

Business people embrace new innovations as a way to adjust and remain serious. They stay informed about innovative progressions pertinent to their industry and investigate their likely applications. Business visionaries will take on and incorporate new innovations into their activities, cycles, or items. By embracing new advancements, business visionaries influence their advantages, improve effectiveness, and drive development.

Reflecting and Reconsidering:

Business people grasp the significance of reflection and reexamination. They put away the opportunity to think about their encounters, triumphs, and disappointments. Business people reconsider their systems, objectives, and needs to guarantee arrangement with their vision. By reflecting and reexamining, business people gain lucidity, refine their methodologies, and settle on informed choices that drive their enterprising excursion forward.

Consistent learning and variation are fundamental parts of reasoning like a business person. Fruitful business visionaries embrace a development mentality, focus on long lasting learning, and look for different points of view. They adjust to showcase shifts, embrace disappointment as learning an open door, and examine and repeat. Business people construct an organization of coaches and counselors, ceaselessly work on their cycles and frameworks, and embrace new innovations. By reflecting and reexamining, business people refine their methodologies and guarantee arrangement with their vision and objectives. Through nonstop learning and variation, business people cultivate dexterity, development, and flexibility, situating themselves for long haul outcomes in the always changing pioneering scene.

CONCLUSION

Congrats! You have left on an extraordinary excursion investigating the complexities of reasoning like a business visionary. All through this book, we have dug into the fundamental parts of business venture, from distinguishing valuable open doors and embracing dangers to creating successful techniques and building solid organizations. We have investigated the significance of promoting, scaling, and consistent learning, among other indispensable points.

Thinking like a business visionary isn't restricted to beginning a business or chasing after a particular undertaking. It is an outlook — an approach to seeing the world, moving toward difficulties, and quickly jumping all over chances. A mentality embraces innovativeness, versatility, and a tenacious quest for development and effect.

As you ponder the information and bits of knowledge acquired from this book, I urge you to encapsulate the quintessence of the enterprising mentality in your own life, whether you are a trying business person, a carefully prepared entrepreneur, or basically somebody looking to develop a pioneering way to deal with life.

To think like a business visionary means to encourage a development mentality that embraces constant learning and variation. It implies remaining inquisitive, looking for assorted points of view, and remaining receptive to showcase moves and arising patterns. It implies embracing disappointment as a significant learning open door and moving toward difficulties with flexibility and determination.

Thinking like a business visionary additionally involves the capacity to distinguish and jump all over chances. It implies fostering a sharp feeling of perception, developing a mentality of advancement, and keeping a persevering drive to make an incentive for other people. It implies moving toward issues as any open doors, tracking down intelligent fixes, and proceeding with carefully thought out plans of action.

Besides, thinking like a business person includes major areas of strength for building and encouraging cooperative connections. It implies perceiving the force of cooperation, looking for mentorship and direction, and sustaining a strong biological system. It implies taking part in significant associations and utilizing the aggregate knowledge and assets of an organization to enhance your effect.

As you set out on your enterprising excursion, recall that it isn't simply about monetary achievement or accomplishing individual objectives. Genuine pioneering thinking envelops a more extensive reason — a promise to having a beneficial outcome on the planet. It is tied in with making an incentive for other people, taking care of significant issues, and leaving an enduring effect on people, networks, and society all in all.

All in all, thinking like a business person is a long lasting pursuit. An outlook rises above enterprises, disciplines, and conditions. It is about persistently developing, adjusting, and pushing limits. It is tied in with rocking the boat, embracing advancement, and staying enduring despite misfortune.

I trust that this book has filled in as a significant aide on your excursion to thinking like a business person. May it rouse and engage you to embrace the pioneering mentality, open your actual potential, and make a significant and effective heritage.

Keep in mind, the pioneering venture is loaded up with exciting bends in the road, triumphs and disappointments, yet it is through embracing the enterprising mentality that you will track down the flexibility, imagination, and assurance expected to explore the always changing scene of business.

Presently, equipped with the information and bits of knowledge acquired from this book, go forward and allow your enterprising soul to take off. Think beyond practical boundaries, make a move, and have an effect. The world requirements more business people like you — visionaries, trend-setters, and changemakers

.Much thanks to you for going along with me on this edifying excursion. Here's to thinking like a business visionary and embracing an existence of direction, enthusiasm, and probability. Go forward and leave behind a legacy!